# Bee Catastrophe
## We'll Miss Them When They're Gone

By Marta Magellan

Illustrated by Mauro Magellan

**Catastrophe:**
an event causing great and often sudden damage or suffering; a disaster.

Eifrig Publishing LLC
Berlin  Lemont

*At Eifrig Publishing, our motto is our mission —
"Good for our kids, good for our Earth, and good for our communities."
We are passionate about helping kids develop into caring, creative, thoughtful
individuals who possess positive self-images, celebrate differences, and practice
inclusion. Our books promote social and environmental consciousness and
empower children as they grow in their communities.*

www.eifrigpublishing.com

© 2023 Marta Magellan
Printed in the United States of America

All rights reserved. This publication is protected by Copyright, and
permission should be obtained from the publisher prior to any prohibited
reproduction, storage in a retrieval system, or transmission in any form
or by any means, electronic, mechanical, photocopying, recording, or
likewise.

Published by Eifrig Publishing,
PO Box 66, Lemont, PA 16851, USA
Knobelsdorffstr. 44, 14059 Berlin, Germany.

For information regarding permission, write to:
Rights and Permissions Department,
Eifrig Publishing,
PO Box 66, Lemont, PA 16851, USA.
permissions@eifrigpublishing.com, +1-888-340-6543

Library of Congress Cataloging-in-Publication Data
Magellan, Marta
Bee Catastrophe, We'll Miss Them When They're Gone/
by Marta Magellan, illustrated by Mauro Magellan
p. cm.

Paperback: ISBN 978-1-63233-360-5
Hardcover: ISBN 978-1-63233-361-2
Ebook:     ISBN 978-1-63233-362-9

[1. Nature - Juvenile Nonfiction. 2. Animals - Bees, Honey Bees,
Pollinators, Insects - Juvenile Nonfiction
I. Magellan, Mauro, ill. II. Title

27 25 25 24 2023
5 4 3 2 1

Printed on recycled PCW acid-free paper. ∞

As always, in honor of Sammy Joe Schnall

Dedicated to Leah, Sebastian, and Juniper

Bee Catastrophe was vetted by Kim Robertson, Master Beekeeper, Florida Master Gardener, and staff member of Bees Beyond Borders and endorsed by David Hackenberg, commercial beekeeper and co-chairman of the Honey Bee Health Advisory Board.

For centuries, fields hummed with the sound of insects. Crickets chirped, katydids trilled, and honey bees buzzed.

People and animals ate the honey. Some animals even ate the bees. And all types of bees did their part to pollinate plants and help them grow.

Here's the catastrophe: Bee by bee, colony by colony, these buzzers have been disappearing.

One day, a beekeeper in Florida went to check on his hives.

Dead bees. Lots of them.

A few years back, he was the first beekeeper to report the loss of most of his bees.

The worker bees had abandoned his hives, causing the hive to fail.

Did they fly off again?

Not this time.

The worker bees were still in the hive, dead.

The beekeeper wondered if an animal attacked it to get to the honey.

No, the honey was untouched.

Maybe it was the varroa mite, an eight-legged crab-like creature that lives off bees.

He examined the bees.

No mites.

It was a mystery.

But why should we care?

Varroa Mite

With help from bats, birds, and lizards, most of the food we eat depends on insects to grow.

They do that by spreading pollen, a yellow powder inside the flower.

Butterflies, moths, beetles, and dragonflies all help spread pollen from blossom to blossom.

But bees are the superstars.

When a bee lands on a flower,
pollen sticks to the hairs of its body.

The pollen gets rubbed off on other flowers, and bingo! A seed is formed.

Seeds cause more flowers and plants to grow.

Without bees, supermarkets would be almost empty.

14

Imagine your life without bees.

Do you like apples and apple pie? Strawberries and strawberry jam? Lemons and lemonade? How about almonds and almond milk?

Too bad. They'd be the first to go.

Vegetables like broccoli, zucchini, carrots, and pumpkin?

They'd go next.

The foods we like most would cost a fortune, if you could find them at all.

Like ice cream, for example.

Dairy cows eat alfalfa, which depends on bees.

So no cheese, no whipped cream, no yogurt... no more ice cream!

To avoid this catastrophe, the mystery of the dying bees had to be solved.

Finally, scientists figured it out.

A chemical bug killer or pesticide used on food crops
was damaging the bees.

The group of chemicals has a very long name: neonicotinoids
(we just say neonics for short).

This pesticide stays in the plant as it grows.

And a terrible thing happens to bees that land on treated plants.

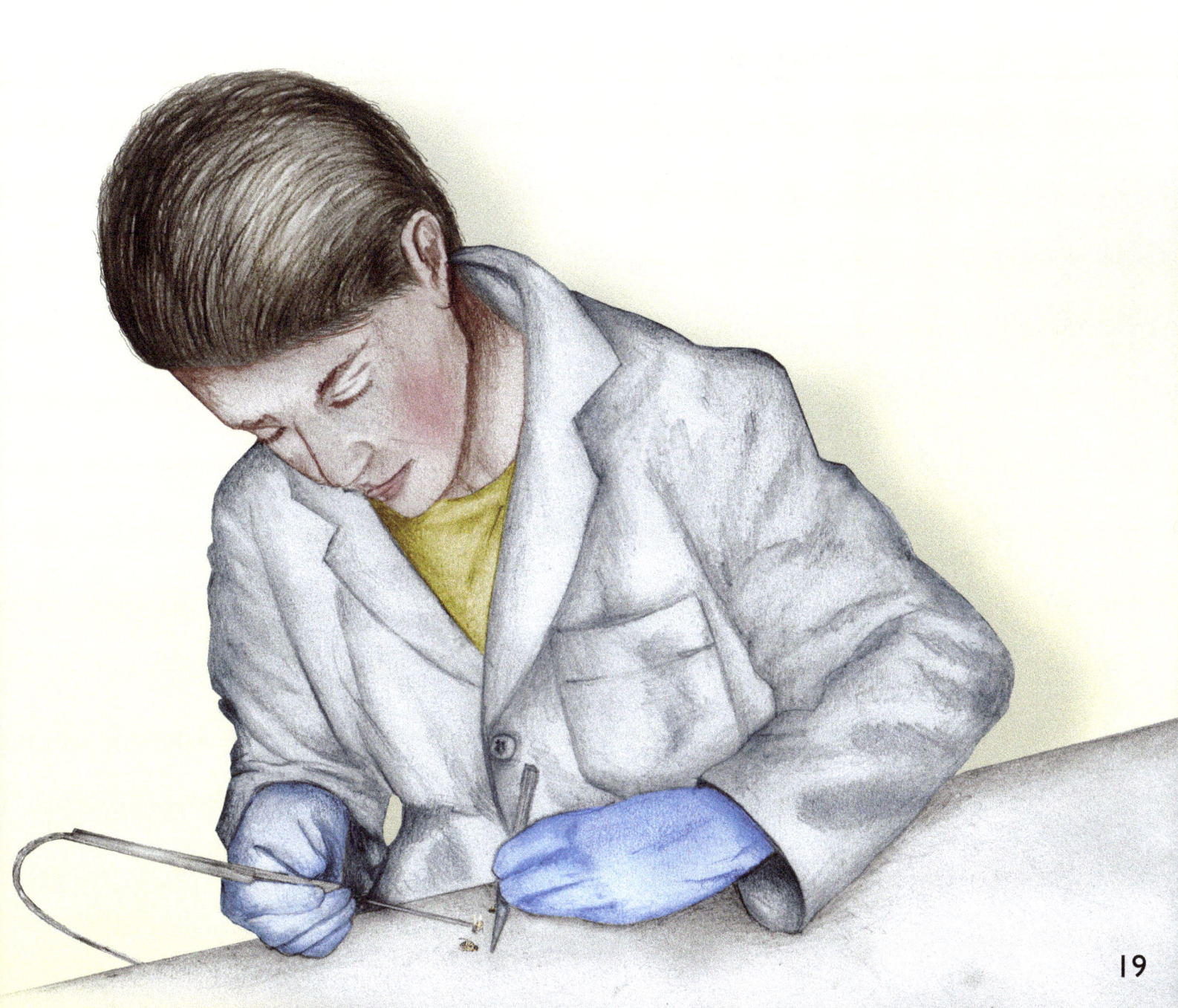

The bees become paralyzed and die.

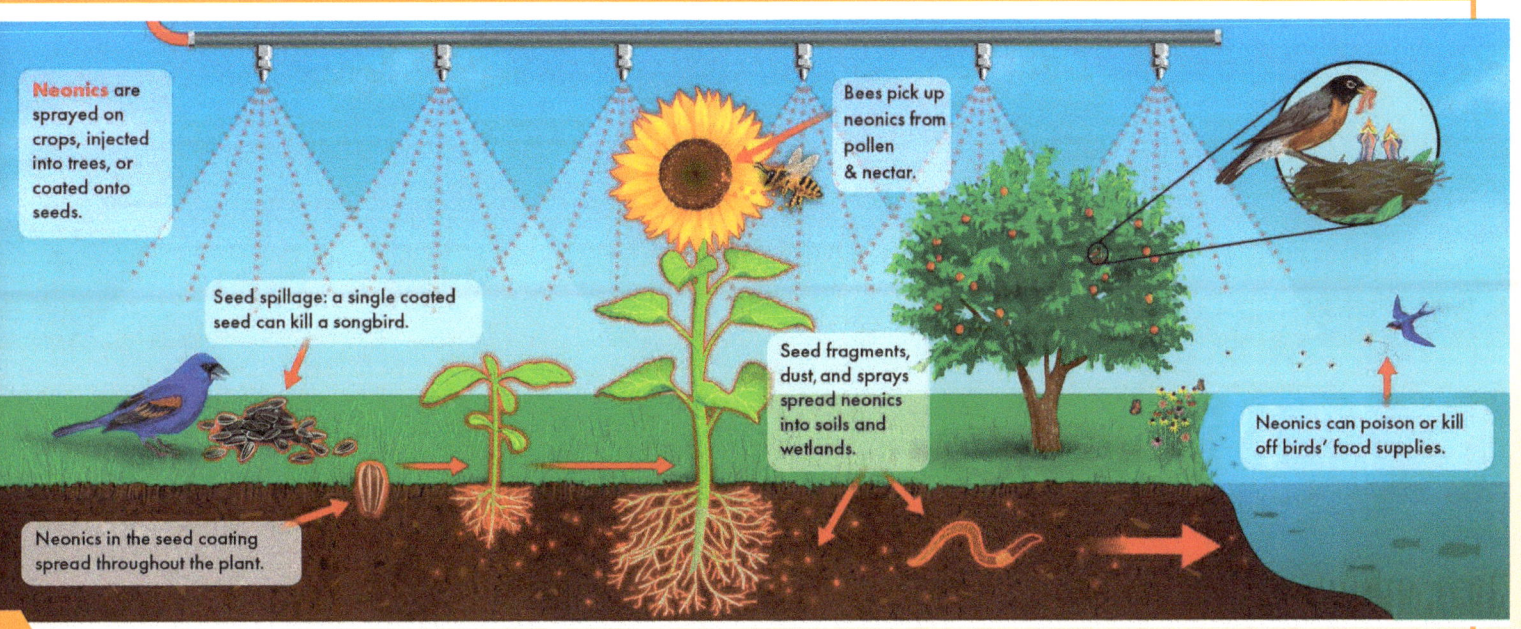

"Neonics and Birds" 2016. American Bird Conservancy. Accessed 18 Aug. 2022. abcbirds.org/neonics

Neonics hurt birds and fish, too. Most of the seeds planted for food are coated with neonics.

Even the seeds you buy for your garden may be sprayed with this super-poison. And they work no better than safer pesticides. Many food safety organizations wanted to ban neonics altogether.

It didn't happen.

But the catastrophe had to be stopped.

Farmers needed to get rid of pests, but they didn't want to kill bees, too.

So they began to spray only at times when the bees were not active, like at sunset.

Many farmers who grew food crops like wheat and soybeans planted hedges of wild shrubs along their borders. That way, bees would have a place to find nectar and might stay away from sprayed crops.

That slowed the deaths but not enough.

We still notice mosquitoes flitting, cockroaches scurrying, and flies flying.

Look-alike invasive yellow jackets make us think a lot of bees are still buzzing.

But no.

Bees, all kinds of bees, are disappearing faster than ever.

And they need our help.

It will be a catastrophe if we let them die because...

...we'll miss them when they're gone.

But turn the page for ways you can help avoid a bee catastrophe.

# How to Avoid a Bee Catastrophe

**Target your yard:** Your yard is the best place to help bees survive. Plant native flowers and vegetables. Bees prefer blue, yellow, purple, and white flowers. Avoid planting double-flowering varieties. They have less pollen, and it can be harder for the bees to access them with extra petals in the way. Stick close to the original flower form instead of going fancy with hybrids. The bees will thank you for it. But most of all, make sure plants are native to the area you live in.

**Start a school garden:** If there is room at your school, ask your teachers if your class can plant a garden for bees and other pollinators. Tell them it's a great learning opportunity.

**Library gardens:** Who doesn't love a butterfly garden? Some libraries, like the Coral Gables Public Library in Florida have started butterfly gardens on their property. Ask the library director where you live if they can start such a program, adding bee-friendly plants, of course.

**No pesticides:** Ask the adults in your life to avoid using any herbicides or pesticides like glyphosate (Roundup). It's dangerous for bees and people. When you buy seeds, make sure they are NOT treated with any type of neonics, which are usually listed as "systemic pesticides."

**Organic fruit and vegetables:** Ask your parents to buy organic fruit and vegetables if they are affordable where you live.

# Some Cool Facts About Bees

- There are 20,000 species of bees, some live in colonies and others are solitary (alone).

- A predatory wasp, the yellow jacket, is often mistaken for a bee when not seen up close. They are aggressive and much more likely to sting than bees.

- Only the honey bees makes honey, and it takes 12 worker bees their entire lifetime to make one teaspoon of honey.

- The queen bee is so important, commercial beekeepers buy new healthy ones for their hives every year.

- Social bees communicate with each other. They do a cool dance called the waggle, which tells other bees where to find nectar or a new nest.

- Bees are cold-blooded. They shiver to generate heat.

- Flowers have male and female parts. Bees carry pollen from the male to the female to make seeds.

- Varroa mites are the world's most destructive pest of western honey bees. Chemicals to control this pest have caused problems, so beekeepers have turned to non-chemical methods in recent years.

- Bees brush pollen to their back legs and squeeze it into something called a basket to take back to the hive. The orange sacs look like two little saddlebags.

Bee vs. Yellow Jacket

Bee carrying pollen

# Acknowledgements

Many thanks to the organizations involved in the creation of this book: the St. Augustine Garden Club, the Nature Detectives Workshop, the Sisterhood of the Traveling Plants, the St. Johns County Public Library System, Bees Beyond Borders, and Penny Eifrig for promoting books that are good for our earth and our children.

Thank you to the SCBWI's Miami Critique Group: Silvia Lopez, Paul and Donna Kurtz, Debbie Wanninkhof, Sara Echenique, Lana Montalban, Ana Siqueira, and all who gave me feedback.

Thanks also to my 12X12 nonfiction critique group: Christina Iverson, Jackie Boice, Leslie Ross Degnan, Kimberly Marcus, Songju Daemicke.

And a very special thank-you to Cathy and Bill Snyder for their generous hospitality and enthusiasm for education and to Lucy Crawford whose zest for nature and pollinators made her a great addition to my presentations at the Ponte Vedra Library.

## Selected References

Ellis, James. D. and C. M. Zettel Nalen. "Varroa, *Varroa Destructor* Anderson and Trueman (Arachnida: Acari: Varroidae)." University of Florida IFAS Extension. Publication #EENY-473. 19 June 2022.

Hirsch, R. *Where Have All the Bees Gone? Pollinators in Crisis*. Minneapolis: Twenty-First Century Books. 2020.

Kessler, S., Tiedeken, E., Simcock, K. *et al*. Bees prefer foods containing neonicotinoid pesticides. *Nature* **521**, 74–76 (2015). https://doi.org/10.1038/nature14414

Weidensaul, S. "Neonic Nation." *Living Bird*. Cornell Lab of Ornithology. Vol. 41, Issue 3, Summer 2022.

EPA. United States Environmental Protection Agency. "EPA Action to Protect Pollinators." 20 Jul 2022. Accessed 13 Aug. 2022.

Wood, J. "US beekeepers continue to report high colony loss rates, no clear progress toward improvement." *The Newsroom*. College of Agriculture, Auburn University. 25 June 2021.

Photo Images from wikicommons

# About the Author and Illustrator

Marta Magellan and Mauro Magellan are a brother and sister team. Born in Rio de Janeiro, Brazil they came to the United States as children. After having published separately for many years, they now collaborate on picture books.

Marta taught Composition, Creative Writing, and Survey of Children's Literature at Miami Dade College, where she was a full professor and literary magazine adviser. Her love for children and nature has produced several children's books with emphasis on ecology and conservation.

Mauro is an illustrator, graphic artist, and rock and blues musician who has illustrated children's books as well as nonfiction for adults. He has written and illustrated various children's books of his own, including *Felicia and the Rat* and *Louie and That Dog*, both with original music.

Contact the author and illustrator at: www.martamagellan.com

*Bee Catastrophe* was designed by Rachel Magellan. She is a professional designer living in Wisconsin.

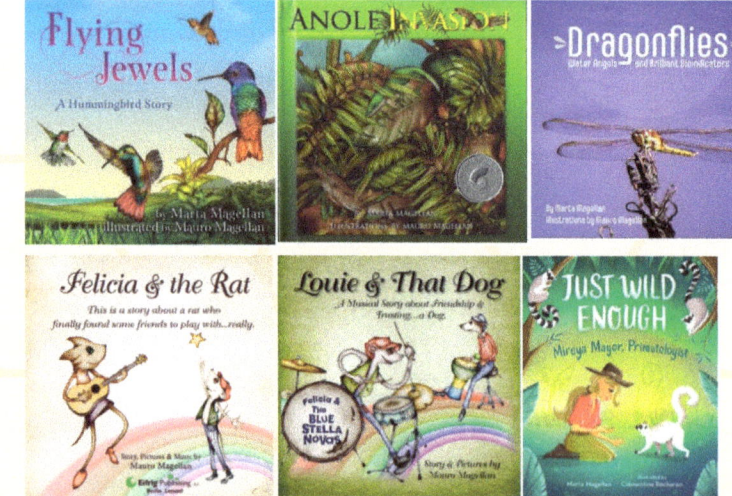

www.ingramcontent.com/pod-product-compliance
Lightning Source LLC
Chambersburg PA
CBHW040010080526
44586CB00028B/2960